Making Choices
in my COMMUNITY

By Diane Lindsey Reeves

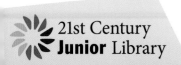

21st Century
Junior Library

Published in the United States of America by
Cherry Lake Publishing
Ann Arbor, Michigan
www.cherrylakepublishing.com

Reading Adviser: Marla Conn MS. Ed., Literacy specialist, Read-Ability, Inc.

Photo Credits: Cover, © 2xSamara.com; page 4, © Joel Wollwerth; page 6, © Paul Vasarhelyi; page 8, © ND700; page 10, © Rawpixel.com; page 12, © Rawpixel.com; page 14, © Dan Holm; page 16, © Golden Pixels LLC; page 18, © Viacheslav Nikolaenko; page 20, © Jack Frog. *Source: Shutterstock.*

Library of Congress Cataloging-in-Publication Data
CIP data has been filed and is available at catalog.loc.gov.

Cherry Lake Publishing would like to acknowledge the work of The Partnership for 21st Century Skills.
Please visit *www.p21.org* for more information.

Printed in the United States of America.

CONTENTS

5 **Home Sweet Home**

11 **People in My Community**

19 **Good Neighbors**

22 My Smart Choices

23 Glossary

24 Index

24 About the Author

Communities are where people live, work, learn, and play.

Home Sweet Home

Welcome to your community! This is where you live with your family. It is where you go to school. It is where you play and make friends.

Think about your community. What do you like about where you live?

In this book, you will make choices. Think of ways you can be part of your community!

My Choice!

- Enjoy my community
- Avoid my community

Families enjoy spending time together in their communities.

Communities come in all shapes and sizes. They may be big or small. Some are in cities. Some are in **suburbs** or in small towns. Communities have houses, apartments, and **townhomes**. People call all of these places home.

People who live together in communities are called neighbors. Good neighbors make good communities.

Do you know your neighbors?

My Choice!

- Be friendly with my neighbors
- **Ignore** my neighbors

Rules keep people safe.

All communities have rules. Rules help people be good neighbors.

Every rule has a reason. Rules remind people how to get along. They help us make good choices. They help us take care of our communities.

Does your community have rules? What are they? Why are they important?

My Choice!

- Obey the rules in my community
- Disobey the rules in my community

Communities include all kinds of neighbors.

People in My Community

All kinds of people live in your community. Some are a lot like you. But look closer.

Some people have different skin color. Some speak different languages. Some are a lot older. Some have **disabilities**.

Being kind to others is always a good idea. It is nice to treat everyone with **respect**.

My Choice!

- Treat everyone with kindness and respect
- Only be nice to people who are just like me

There are lots of jobs to do in communities.

Communities need people to do different jobs. People work at hospitals, schools, or offices. Some work at bakeries, grocery stores, or restaurants. Others run businesses or build buildings.

Working together is how communities work best. What if people didn't do their jobs? What would happen?

Your job now is to do your best in school. Are you doing a good job?

My Choice!

- Do a good job in school
- Goof around and don't do my homework

First responders protect communities.

People in communities **protect** each other. Police, firefighters, and **paramedics** are called first responders. They **rescue** people when they need help the most.

First responders have tough jobs. They often put themselves in danger to help others. People in communities can make their jobs easier. Obeying laws is one way.

Has a first responder ever helped your family? How did you treat them?

My Choice!

- Show respect to first responders
- Refuse to listen to first responders

People in communities share pools, playgrounds, and other fun places.

People in communities share lots of things. They share streets and sidewalks. They share restaurants and stores. They share libraries and schools. Hospitals and places to **worship** are for everyone, too.

Communities also share fun places to play. Pools, playgrounds, and parks are places neighbors enjoy together.

What fun places do you share in your community?

My Choice!

- Share community places
- Be selfish about community places

Good neighbors take care of each other.

Good Neighbors

Sometimes people in communities need extra help. They may be sick. They may have disabilities. Certain **tasks** may be too hard. People may need jobs or even food.

Communities pitch in to help each other. That's what good neighbors do.

Do your neighbors need help? What can you do for them?

My Choice!

- Be a good neighbor
- Just look out for myself

Friendly communities make everyone feel welcome.

People make communities better by being kind. They also help out. How can you make your community a good place to call home?

My Choice!

- Care about my community
- Just do my own thing

MY SMART CHOICES

Write a story about two different days. One day you make smart choices in your community. The other day you don't. How are the two days different? Which day did you enjoy the most?

GLOSSARY

disabilities (dis-uh-BIL-ih-teez) things that keep someone from being able to do the things that most people can do; this is usually because of an illness or injury

ignore (ig-NOR) to pay no attention to something

paramedics (par-uh-MED-iks) people trained to give medical help but who are not doctors or nurses

protect (pruh-TEKT) to keep someone safe from harm

rescue (res kyoo) to save someone who is in danger or in a difficult situation

respect (rəˈSPEK) to show admiration or high regard for someone

suburbs (SUHB-urbz) neighborhoods that are located close to a city

tasks (TASKS) work that needs to be done

townhomes (TOUN-hohmz) a house that is usually two stories tall and connected to a similar house

worship (WUR-ship) the act of honoring and showing love to God

INDEX

A
apartments, 7

B
basketball, 18

C
cities, 7
community helpers, 12
condos, 7

D
disabilities, 19

F
firefighters, 15
first responders, 15

H
houses, 7

M
My Choice, 5, 7, 9, 11, 13, 15, 17, 18, 21,
My Smart Choices, 22

N
neighbors, 4

P
paramedics, 15
police, 15

R
rules, 9

S
soccer, 18
suburb, 7
swimming, 18

T
T-ball, 18
tennis, 18
townhomes, 7

ABOUT THE AUTHOR

When Diane Lindsey Reeves isn't writing children's books, she chooses to play with her four grandchildren. She lives in Cary, North Carolina and Washington, D.C.